The Quotable
Robert F. Kennedy

All great questions must be raised by great voices, and the greatest voice is the voice of the people-speaking out-in prose, or painting or poetry or music; speaking out-in homes and halls, streets and farms, courts and cafes-let that voice speak and the stillness you hear will be the gratitude of mankind. **Robert F. Kennedy 10th Anniversary Convocation Center for Study of Democratic Institutions of the Fund for the Republic, New York City, January 22, 1963**.

More and more of our children are estranged, alienated in the literal sense, almost unreachable by the familiar premises and arguments of our adult world. And the task of leadership, the first task of concerned people, is not to condemn or castigate or deplore-it is to search out the reason for disillusionment and alienation, the rationale of protest and dissent-perhaps, indeed, to learn from it. And we will learn most, I think, from the minority who most sharply articulate their criticism of our ways. And we may find that we learn most of all from those political and social dissenters whose different with us are most grave; for among the young as among adults, the sharpest criticism often goes hand in hand with the deepest idealism and love of country. **Robert F. Kennedy, Americans for Democratic Action, Philadelphia, Pennsylvania February 24, 1967.**

Justice delayed is democracy denied. **Robert F. Kennedy**

The problem of power is how to achieve its responsible use rather than its irresponsible and indulgent use - of how to get men of power to live for the public rather than off the public. **Robert F. Kennedy**

Few men are willing to brave the disapproval of their fellows, the censure of their colleagues, the wrath of their society. Moral courage is a rarer commodity than bravery in battle or great intelligence. Yet it is the one essential, vital quality for those who seek to change a world which yields most painfully to change. **Robert F. Kennedy, 1966**

Few will have the greatness to bend history itself; but each of us can work to change a small portion of events, and in the total of all those acts will be written the history of this generation. **Robert F. Kennedy**

There are those that look at things the way they are, and ask why? I dream of things that never were, and ask why not. **Robert F. Kennedy**

What is objectionable, what is dangerous, about extremists is not that they are extreme, but that they are intolerant. The evil is not what they say about their cause, but what they say about their opponents. **Robert F. Kennedy**

Those who dare to fail miserably can achieve greatly. **Robert F. Kennedy**

The free way of life proposes ends, but it does not prescribe means. **Robert F. Kennedy**

Few will have the greatness to bend history itself; but each of us can work to change a small portion of events, and in the total; of all those acts will be written the history of this generation. **Robert F. Kennedy**

It is from numberless diverse acts of courage and belief that human history is shaped. Each time a man stands up for an ideal, or acts to improve the lot of others, or strikes out against injustice, he sends forth a tiny ripple of hope, and crossing each other from a million different centers of energy and daring those ripples build a current which can sweep down the mightiest walls of oppression and injustice. **Robert F. Kennedy**

Whenever men take the law into their own hands, the loser is the law. And when the law loses, freedom languishes. **Robert F. Kennedy**

One-fifth of the people are against everything all the time. **Robert F. Kennedy**

Few are willing to brave the disapproval of their fellows, the censure of their colleagues, the wrath of their society. Moral courage is a rarer commodity than bravery in battle or great intelligence. Yet it is the one essential, vital quality for those who seek to change a world that yields most painfully to change. And I believe that in this generation those with the courage to enter the moral conflict will find themselves with companions in every corner of the globe. **Robert F. Kennedy**

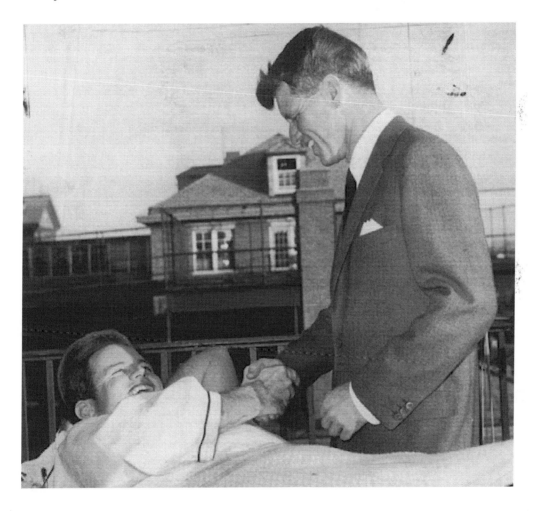

For the fortunate among us, there is the temptation to follow the easy and familiar paths of personal ambition and financial success so grandly spread before those who enjoy the privilege of education. But that is not the road history has marked out for us. Like it or not, we live in times of danger and uncertainty. But they are also more open to the creative energy of men than any other time in history. All of us will ultimately be judged, and as the years pass we will surely judge ourselves on the effort we have contributed to building a new world society and the extent to which our ideals and goals have shaped that event. **Robert F. Kennedy**

The future does not belong to those who are content with today, apathetic toward common problems and their fellow man alike, timid and fearful in the face of new ideas and bold projects. Rather it will belong to those who can blend vision, reason and courage in a personal commitment to the ideals and great enterprises of American Society. Our future may lie beyond our vision, but it is not completely beyond our control. It is the shaping impulse of America that neither fate nor nature nor the irresistible tides of history, but the work of our own hands, matched to reason and principle, that will determine our destiny. There is pride in that, even arrogance, but there is also experience and truth. In any event, it is the only way we can live. That is the way he lived. That is what he leaves us. My brother need not be idealized, or enlarged in death beyond what he was in life; to be remembered simply as a good and decent man, who saw wrong and tried to right it, saw suffering and tried to heal it, saw war and tried to stop it.

Those of us who loved him and who take him to his rest today, pray that what he was to us and what he wished for others will someday come to pass for all the world. **Robert F. Kennedy**

 As he said many times, in many parts of this nation, to those he touched and who sought to touch him: Some men see things as they are and say why. I dream things that never were and say why not. **Edward Kennedy eulogy for Robert F. Kennedy**

We know that it is law which enables men to live together, that creates order out of chaos. We know that law is the glue that holds civilization together. And we know that if one man's rights are denied, the rights of all others are endangered **Robert F. Kennedy, 1961**

To meet the challenge of our times, so that we can later look back upon this era not as one of which we need be ashamed but as a turning point on the way to a better America, we must first defeat the enemy within. **Robert F. Kennedy**

It is the shaping impulse of America that neither fate nor nature nor the irresistible tides of history, but the work of our own hands, matched to reason and principle, which can determine destiny. There is pride in that, even arrogance, but there is also experience and truth. In any event, it is the only way we can live. **Robert F. Kennedy Address, China Conference, University of Chicago, February 8, 1967.**

What matters about this country cannot be put into simple slogans; it is a process, a way of doing things and dealing with people., a way of life. There are two major ways to communicate what this country is really about: to bring people here, or to send Americans abroad. **Robert F. Kennedy Address, Sixth Annual West Side Community Conference, Columbia University, New York City, March 12, 1966.**

This is the breaking of a man's spirit by denying him the chance to stand as a father and as a man among other men. And this too afflicts us all. **Robert F. Kennedy**

Are we like the God of the Old Testament, that we in Washington can decide which cities, towns, and hamlets in Vietnam will be destroyed? Do we have to accept that? I don't think we do. I think we can do something about it. **Robert F. Kennedy**

In many ways Wall Street is closer to London than it is to Harlem, a few miles uptown; Scarsdale is often closer to Paris than to Selma, Alabama; and Americans in Appalachia are in many ways closer to Favelas of Rio de Janeiro than they are to society in which you and I live. **Robert F. Kennedy May 2, 1965.**

Challenge. My faith is that Americans are not an inert people. My conviction is that we are rising as a people to confront the hard challenges of our age-and that we know that the hardest challenges are often those within ourselves. My confidence is that, as we strive constantly to meet the exacting standard of our national tradition, we will liberate a moral emery within our nation which will transform America's role and America's influence throughout the world-and that upon this release of energy depends the world's hope for peace, freedom and justice everywhere. **Robert F. Kennedy Address, Joint Defense Appeal of the American Jewish Committee and the Anti-Defamation League of B;nai B'rith, Chicago, Illinois, June 21, 1961 .**

...Time and time again the American people, facing danger and seemingly insurmountable odds, have mobilized the ingenuity, resourcefulness, strength, and bravery to meet the situation and triumph. In this long and critical struggle, the American System of free enterprise must be our major weapon. We must continue to prove to the world that we can provide a rising standard of living for all men without the loss of civil rights or human dignity to any man. **Robert F. Kennedy Speech, Chicago, August 1963**.

The great challenge to all Americans-indeed to all free men and women-is to maintain loyalty to truth; to maintain loyalty to free institutions; to maintain loyalty to freedom as a basic human value, and above all else to keep in our hearts and minds the tolerance and mutual trust that have been the genius of American life throughout our history. **Speech, the National Conference of Christians and Jews Dinner, Cleveland, Ohio, December 3, 1961.**

The challenge of politics and public service is to discover what is interfering with justice and dignity for the individual here and now, and then to decide swiftly upon the appropriate remedies. **Speech, Athens, Georgia, May 6, 1961.**

On this generation of Americans falls the full burden of providing the world that we really mean it when we say all men are created free and equal before the law. All of us might wish at times that we lived in a more tranquil world, but we don't. And if our times are difficult and perplexing, so are they challenging and filled with opportunity. **Speech, Law Day Exercises of the University of Georgetown Law School, May 6, 1961.**

It is not easy, in the middle of one's life or political career, to say that the old horizons are too limited-that our education must begin again. But neither are the challenges ahead easy. The best responses will not be easily found; nor once found, will they command unanimous agreement. But the possibilities of greatness are equal to the difficulty of the challenge. **Address, Retail, Wholesale and Department Store Union Convention, Miami Beach, Florida, May 27, 1966.**

I don't see anything wrong with giving him (Robert Kennedy) a little legal experience before he goes out to practice law. **John F. Kennedy**

The path of innovation is never easy. Change is always painful. But it is the only path with the promise of saving our cities, the only path with the potential of bringing forth the resources needed for the task ahead. In our central cities are millions of Americans who have too long been denied a share in the American dream. And the gap is widening. Therefore we must join together-the people of the neighborhood, government, private enterprise, foundations, and universities-in an effort of unprecedented scope. The future of our nation demands that.
Model City Conference, Buffalo, New York, January 20, 1967.

In such a fantastic and dangerous world-we will not find answers in old dogmas, by repeating outworn slogans, or fighting on ancient battlegrounds against fading enemies long after the real struggle has moved on. We ourselves must change to master change. We must rethink al our told ideas and beliefs before they capture and destroy us. And for those answers American must look to its young people, the children of this time of change. And we look especially to that privileged minority of educated men who are students of America. **Speech, Worthington, Minnesota, September 17, 1966.**

The future does not belong to those who are content with today, apathetic towards common problems and their fellow man alike, timid and fearful in the face of new ideas and bold projects. Rather it will belong to those who can blend passion, reason and courage in a personal commitment to the ideals an great enterprises of American society. It will belong to those who see that wisdom can only emerge from the clash of contending views, the passionate expression of deep and hostile beliefs. Plato said: A life without criticism is not worth living.
Address, Berkeley Campus, University of California, October 22, 1966.

To say that the future will be different from the present and past may be hopelessly self-evident. I must observe regretfully, however, that in politics it can be heresy. It can be denounced as radicalism or branded as subversion. There are people in every time and every land who want to stop history in its tracks. They fear the future, mistrust the present and invoke the security of a comfortable past, which in fact, never existed. It hardly seems necessary to point out in the United States, of all places, that change, although it involves risk, is the law of life. **Speech, New York, May 20, 1964.**

Progress. Progress is a nice word. But change is its motivator. And change has its enemies. **Chicago, August, 1963.**

The plight of the cities-the physical decay and human despair that pervades them-is the great internal problem of the American nation, a challenge which must be met. The peculiar genius of America has been its ability, in the face of such challenges, to summon all our resources of mind and body, to focus these resources, and our attention and effort, in whatever amount is necessary to solve the deepest and most resistant problems. That is the commitment and the spirit required in our cities today. **Model City Conference, Buffalo, New York, January 20, 1967.**

The city is not just housing and stores. It is not just education and employment, parks and theatres, banks and shops. It is a place where men should be able to live in dignity and security and harmony, where the great achievements of modern civilization and the ageless pleasures afforded by natural beauty should be available to all. If this is what we want-and this is what we must want if en are to be free for that pursuit of happiness which was the earliest promise of the American nation-we will need more than poverty programs, housing programs and employment programs, although we will need all of these. We will needs an outpouring of imagination, ingenuity, discipline and hard work unmatched since the first adventures set out to conquer the wilderness. For the problem is the largest we have ever known. And we confront an urban wilderness more formidable and resistant and in some ways more frightening than the wilderness faced by the pilgrims or the pioneers. **Remarks before the Subcommittee on Executive Reorganization of the Committee on Government Operations of the United States Senate, August 15, 1966.**

It is from numberless diverse acts of courage and belief that human history is shaped. Each time a man stands up for an ideal, or acts to improve the lot of other, or strikes out against injustice, he send forth a tiny ripple of hope, and crossing each other from a million different centers of energy and daring those ripples build a current which can sweep down the mightiest walls of oppression and resistance. **Address Day of Affirmation, University of Capetown, June 6, 1966.**

Democracy is no easy form of government. Few nations have been able to sustain it. For it requires that we take the chances of freedom; that the liberating play of reason be brought to bear on events filled with passion; that dissent be allowed to make its appeal for acceptance; that men chance in error in their search for the truth. **Statement on Vietnam, February 19, 1966.**

We know full well the faults of our democracy-the handicaps of freedom-the inconvenience of dissent. But I know of no American who would not rather be a servant in the imperfect house of Freedom, than be a master of all the empires of tyranny. **Address, the 120th Anniversary Dinner of B'nai B'rith, Chicago, October 13, 1963.**

It is not enough to allow dissent. We must demand it. For there is much to dissent from. We dissent from the fact that millions are trapped in poverty while the nation grows rich. We dissent from the conditions and hatred which deny a full life to our fellow citizens because of the color of their skin. We dissent from the monstrous absurdity of a world where nations stand poised to destroy one another, and men must kill their fellow men. We dissent from the sight of most of mankind living in poverty, stricken by disease, threatened by hunger and doomed to an early death after a life of unremitting labor. We dissent from cities which blunt our senses and turn the ordinary acts of daily life into a painful struggle. We dissent from the willful, heedless destruction of natural pleasure and beauty. We dissent from all those structures-of technology and of society itself-which strip from the individual the dignity and warmth of sharing in the common tasks of his community and his country. **Address, Berkeley Campus, University of California, October 22, 1966.**

Education is the key to jobs-to income-to human dignity itself...In the last analysis the quality of education is a question of commitment-of whether people like us are willing to go into the classrooms as teachers or parents, as volunteers or just as concerned citizens, to ensure that every child learns to the full limit his capabilities. **Speech, University of Alabama, March 18, 1966.**

I suspect there may always be arguments about what constitutes a higher education, but wise men through the ages have at least been able to agree on its purpose. Its purpose is not only to discipline and instruct, but above all to free the mind-to free it from the darkness, the narrowness, the groundless fears and self-defeating passions of ignorance. You may sometimes regret it, for a free mind insists on seeking out reality, and reality is often a far more painful matter than the soft and comfortable illusions of the intellectually poor. **Speech, Commencement Exercises, Trinity College, Washington, D.C., June 2, 1963.**

The free way of life proposes ends, but it does not prescribe means. It assumes that people, and nations will often think differently, have the full right to do so, and that diversity is the source of progress. It believes that men advance by , by debate, by trial and by error. It believes that the best ideas come, not from edict and ideology, but from free inquiry and free experiment; and it regards dissent not as treason to the state, but as the tested mechanism of social progress. And it knows the diverse nations will find diverse roads to the general goal of political independence and economic growth. It regards the free individual as the source of creativity, and believes that it is the roles of the state to serve him, and not his role to serve the state. **Speech, Chicago, August 1963.**

It is the ideal of freedom which underlines our great concern for civil rights. Nations around the world look to us for leadership not merely by strength of arms, but by the strength of our convictions. We not only want, but we need, the free exercise of rights by every American. We need the strength and talent of every American. We need, in short, to set an example of freedom for the world- and for ourselves. **Address, American Jewish Congress, New York City, October 28, 1962.**

If our Constitution had followed the style of St. Paul, the First Amendment might have concluded-But the greatest of these is speech. In the darkness of tyranny, that is the key to the sunlight. If it is granted, all doors open. If it is withheld, none. **Address, 10th Anniversary Convocation, On freedom of speech, Center for Study of Democratic Institutions of the Fund for the Republic, New York City, January 22, 1963.**

It is not easy to plant trees when we will not live to see their flowering. But that way lies greatness. And in search of greatness we will find it-for ourselves as a nation and a people. **RFK**

We must recognize the full human equality of all our people-before God, before the law, and in the councils of government. We must do this, not because it is economically advantageous-although it is; not because the laws of God and man command it-although they do command it; not because people in other lands wish it so. We must do it for the single and fundamental reason that it is the right thing to do. **RFK**

The first element of individual liberty is the freedom of speech; the right to express and communicate ideas, to set oneself apart from the dumb beasts of field and forest; to recall governments to their duties and obligations; above all, the right to affirm one's membership and allegiance to the body politic-to society-to the men with whom we share our land, our heritage and our children's future. Hand in hand with freedom of speech goes the power to be heard-to share in the decisions of government which shape's men's lives. Everything that make's man's life worthwhile-family, work, education, a place to rear one's children and a place to rest one's head-all this depends on decisions of government; all can be swept away by a government which does not heed the demands of its people. Therefore, the essential humanity of men can be protected and preserves only where government must answer-not just to the wealthy; not just to those of a particular religion, or a particular race; but to all its people. And even government by the consent of the governed, as in our own constitution, must be limited in its power to act against its people so that there may be no interference with the right to worship, or with the security of the home; no arbitrary imposition of pains or penalties by officials high or low; no restriction on the freedom of men to seek education or work or opportunity of any kind, so that each man may become all he is capable of becoming. These are the sacred rights of western society. These were the essential differences between us and Nazi Germany as they were between Athens and Persia. **Address, Day of Affirmation, University of Capetown, June 6, 1966.**

When there were periods of crisis, you stood beside him. When there were periods of happiness, you laughed with him. And when there were periods of sorrow, you comforted him. **Tribute to John F. Kennedy, 1964 Democratic National Convention in Atlantic City August 1964**

What is the price tag on equal justice under law? Has simple justice a price which we as a profession must exact? Is that what we have come to? Is that what we have come to? It is certainly the way the underprivileged, the poor, the helpless regard us. Helplessness does not stem from the absence of theoretical rights. It can stem from an inability to assert real rights. The tenants of slums, and public housing projects, the purchasers from disreputable finance companies, the minority group member who is discriminated against-all these may have legal rights which-I we are candid-remain in the limbo of the law. **Speech, University of Chicago Law School, Chicago, 1964**

The ultimate relationship between justice and law will be an eternal subject for speculation and analysis. But it may be said that in a democratic society law is the form which free men give to justice. The glory of justice and the majesty of the law are created not just by the Constitution-nor by the courts-nor by the officers of the law-nor by the lawyers-but by the men and women who constitute our society-who are protectors of the law as they are themselves protected by the law. **Ceremonies of the Virginia State Bar, Virginia, May 1, 1962.**

Laws and speeches do not build schools. They do not put capable teachers in the schools. And they do not give children the food, the clothing, the books and the encouragement they need if you are to stay in the shiny new school we build. Laws by themselves will not make a land reform-if farmers do not also have access to credit and technical assistance and fertilizers. Laws and economic aid and reforms by themselves will not create jobs-unless someone is determined to use these economic resources to create the jobs. Laws by themselves will not insure farm workers the minimum wage-unless we act to insure that the laws are enforced. And all our economics, social and material progress will be for nothing-if we do not at the same time move toward increasing freedom toward a society where all can freely speak and act to share in the decisions which shape their lives **Catholic University, Rio de Janeiro, November 25, 1965.**

Leadership in freedom depends on fidelity and persistence in those shaping beliefs-democracy, freedom, justice-which men follow not from the enslavement of their bodies but from the compulsion of their hearts. We must cope with real dangers, overcome real obstacles, meet real needs; but always in a way which preserves our own allegiance to the fundamental principles and promises of the American Constitution. Otherwise we will preserve the shadow of progress and security at the expense of the substance of freedom here in American and all around the world. **Speech, Columbus, Ohio, October 8, 1966, Democratic State Committee Dinner.**

It is not given to us to right every wrong, to make perfect all the imperfections of the world. But neither is it given to us to sit content in our storehouses-dieting while others starve, buying 8 million new cars a year while most of the world goes without shoes. We are simply not doing enough. **Senate Speech, July 21, 1966.**

Let none of us forget that we are living in a time of infinite possibilities. Both domestically and in international relations, America has never before in history had a greater chance to fulfill the dreams of men through ages-dreams of individual freedom, national prosperity, and world peace. **The American G.I. Forum, Chicago, Illinois, August 23, 1963.**

Future. Nations, like men, often march to the beat of different drummers, and the precise solutions of the United States can neither be dictated nor transplanted to others. What is important is that all nations must march toward increasing freedom; toward justice for all; toward a society strong and flexible enough to meet the demands of all its own people, and a world of immense and dizzying change. **Day of Affirmation, University of Capetown, June 6, 1966.**

It is the essence of responsibility to put the public good ahead of personal gain... **(1963)**

The responsibility of our time is nothing less than to lead a revolution-a revolution which will be peaceful if we are wise enough; human is we care enough; successful is we are fortunate enough-but a revolution which will come whether we will it or not. We can affect its character: we cannot alter its inevitability...America is, after all, the land of becoming-a continent which will be in ferment as long as it is America, a land which will never cease to change and grow. We are as we act. We are the children and the heirs of revolutions and we fulfill our destiny only as we advance the struggle which began in Santa Fe in 1580, which continued in Philadelphia in 1776 and Caracas in 1811-and which continues today. **Statement Before Peruvian Students, 1965.**

It should be clear that, if one man's rights are denied, the rights of all are in danger-that if one man is denied equal protection of the law, we cannot be sure that we will enjoy freedom of speech or any other of our fundamental rights. **Speech before the Joint Defense Appeal of the American Jewish Committee and the Anti-Defamation League, Chicago, Illinois, June 21,1961.**

Ultimately, America's answer to the intolerant man is diversity, the very diversity which our heritage of religious freedom has inspired. **Robert F. Kennedy**

For all those whose cares have been our concern, the work goes on, the cause endures, the hope still lives and the dream shall never die. **Ted Kennedy**

Love is not an easy feeling to put into words. Nor is loyalty, or trust, or joy. But he was all of these. He loved life completely and he lived it intensely. **Ted Kennedy Eulogy for Robert F. Kennedy at St. Patrick's Cathedral, New York (June 8, 1968.**

My brother need not be idealized or enlarged in death beyond what he was in life, to be remembered as a good and decent man, who saw wrong and tried to right it, saw suffering and tried to heal it, saw war and tried to stop it. **Ted Kennedy Eulogy for Robert F. Kennedy**

There is discrimination in this world and slavery and slaughter and starvation. Governments repress their people; millions are trapped in poverty while the nation grows rich and wealth is lavished on armaments everywhere. These are differing evils, but they are the common works of man. They reflect the imperfection of human justice, the inadequacy of human compassion, our lack of sensibility towards the suffering of our fellows. But we can perhaps remember -- even if only for a time -- that those who live with us are our brothers; that they share with us the same short moment of life; that they seek -- as we do -- nothing but the chance to live out their lives in purpose and happiness, winning what satisfaction and fulfillment they can. **Robert F. Kennedy**

Surely, this bond of common faith, this bond of common goal, can begin to teach us something. Surely, we can learn, at least, to look at those around us as fellow men. And surely we can begin to work a little harder to bind up the wounds among us and to become in our own hearts brothers and countrymen once again. The answer is to rely on youth -- not a time of life but a state of mind, a temper of the will, a quality of imagination, a predominance of courage over timidity, of the appetite for adventure over the love of ease. The cruelties and obstacles of this swiftly changing planet will not yield to the obsolete dogmas and outworn slogans. They cannot be moved by those who cling to a present that is already dying, who prefer the illusion of security to the excitement and danger that come with even the most peaceful progress. **Robert F. Kennedy**

It is a revolutionary world we live in, and this generation at home and around the world has had thrust upon it a greater burden of responsibility than any generation that has ever lived. Some believe there is nothing one man or one woman can do against the enormous array of the world's ills. Yet many of the world's great movements, of thought and action, have flowed from the work of a single man. A young monk began the Protestant reformation; a young general extended an empire from Macedonia to the borders of the earth; a young woman reclaimed the territory of France; and it was a young Italian explorer who discovered the New World, and the 32 year-old Thomas Jefferson who proclaimed that all men are created equal. These men moved the world, and so can we all. Few will have the greatness to bend history itself, but each of us can work to change a small portion of events, and in the total of all those acts will be written the history of this generation. *It is from numberless diverse acts of courage and belief that human history is shaped. Each time a man stands up for an ideal, or acts to improve the lot of others, or strikes out against injustice, he sends forth a tiny ripple of hope, and crossing each other from a million different centers of energy and daring, those ripples build a current that can sweep down the mightiest walls of oppression and resistance. **Robert F. Kennedy**

Others have seen what is and asked why. I have seen what could be and asked why not?. **Robert F. Kennedy**

Don't get mad, get even. **Robert F. Kennedy**

Moral courage is a more rare commodity than bravery in battle or great intelligence. **Robert F. Kennedy**

Fear not the path of truth for the lack of people walking on it. **Robert F. Kennedy**

Only those who dare to fail greatly can ever achieve greatly. **Robert F. Kennedy**

The sharpest criticism often goes hand in hand with the deepest idealism and love of country. **Robert F. Kennedy**

Men without hope, resigned to despair and oppression, do not make revolutions. It is when expectation replaces submission, when despair is touched with the awareness of possibility, that the forces of human desire and the passion for justice are unloosed. **Robert F. Kennedy**

There are those who look at things the way they are, and ask why... I dream of things that never were and ask why not? **Robert F. Kennedy**

Few will have the greatness to bend history; but each of us can work to change a small portion of events, and in the total of all those acts will be written the history of this generation ... It is from numberless diverse acts of courage and belief that human history is thus shaped. Each time a man stands up for an ideal, or acts to improve the lot of others, or strikes out against injustice, he sends forth a tiny ripple of hope, and crossing each other from a million different centers of energy and daring, those ripples build a current which can sweep down the mightiest walls of oppression and resistance. **Robert F. Kennedy**

At the University of Natal in Durban, I was told the church to which most of the white population belongs teaches apartheid as a moral necessity. A questioner declared that few churches allow black Africans to pray with the white because the Bible says that is the way it should be, because God created Negroes to serve. But suppose God is black, I replied. What if we go to Heaven and we, all our lives, have treated the Negro as an inferior, and God is there, and we look up and He is not white? What then is our response? There was no answer. Only silence. **South Africa, June 1966**

Laws can embody standards; governments can enforce laws—but the final task is not a task for government. It is a task for each and every one of us. Every time we turn our heads the other way when we see the law flouted—when we tolerate what we know to be wrong—when we close our eyes and ears to the corrupt because we are too busy, or too frightened—when we fail to speak up and speak out—we strike a blow against freedom and decency and justice. **June 21, 1961**

We must recognize the full human equality of all our people-before God, before the law, and in the councils of government. We must do this, not because it is economically advantageous-although it is; not because the laws of God and man command it-although they do command it; not because people in other lands wish it so. We must do it for the single and fundamental reason that it is the right thing to do **Robert F. Kennedy**

The problem of power is how to achieve its responsible use rather than its irresponsible and indulgent use — of how to get men of power to live for the public rather than off the public. **Robert F. Kennedy**

Too often, we honor swagger and bluster and the wielders of force. Too often we excuse those who are willing to build their own lives from the shattered dreams of other human beings. But this much is clear, Violence breeds violence, repression breeds retaliation, and only a cleansing of our whole society can remove this sickness from our souls. **Robert F. Kennedy**

I think back to what Camus wrote about the fact that perhaps this world is a world in which children suffer, but we can lessen the number of suffering children, and if you do not do this, then who will do this? I'd like to feel that I'd done something to lessen that suffering. **Robert F. Kennedy**

The problem of power is how to achieve its responsible use rather than its irresponsible and indulgent use — of how to get men of power to live for the public rather than off the public. **Robert F. Kennedy**

Every society gets the kind of criminal it deserves. What is equally true is that every community gets the kind of law enforcement it insists on. **Robert F. Kennedy**

Now I can go back to being ruthless again. **Remark on his reputation for ruthlessness after winning his race for a seat in the United States Senate 1965**

A revolution is coming — a revolution which will be peaceful if we are wise enough; compassionate if we care enough; successful if we are fortunate enough — But a revolution which is coming whether we will it or not. We can affect its character; we cannot alter its inevitability. **Robert F. Kennedy**

Gross National Product counts air pollution and cigarette advertising, and ambulances to clear our highways of carnage. It counts special locks for our doors and the jails for the people who break them. It counts the destruction of the redwood and the loss of our natural wonder in chaotic sprawl. It counts napalm and counts nuclear warheads and armored cars for the police to fight the riots in our cities. It counts Whitman's rifle and Speck's knife, and the television programs which glorify violence in order to sell toys to our children. Yet the gross national product does not allow for the health of our children, the quality of their education or the joy of their play. It does not include the beauty of our poetry or the strength of our marriages, the intelligence of our public debate or the integrity of our public officials. It measures neither our wit nor our courage, neither our wisdom nor our learning, neither our compassion nor our devotion to our country, it measures everything in short, except that which makes life worthwhile. And it can tell us everything about America except why we are proud that we are Americans. **Robert F. Kennedy**

Every dictatorship has ultimately strangled in the web of repression it wove for its people, making mistakes that could not be corrected because criticism was prohibited. **Robert F. Kennedy**

For there is another kind of violence, slower but just as deadly destructive as the shot or the bomb in the night. This is the violence of institutions; indifference and inaction and slow decay. This is the violence that afflicts the poor, that poisons relations between men because their skin has different colors. This is the slow destruction of a child by hunger, and schools without books and homes without heat in the winter. **Robert F. Kennedy**

And even government by the consent of the governed, as in our own Constitution, must be limited in its power to act against its people; so that there may be no interference with the right to worship, or with the security of the home; no arbitrary imposition of pains or penalties by officials high or low; no restrictions on the freedom of men to seek education or work or opportunity of any kind, so that each man may become all he is capable of becoming. **Robert F. Kennedy**

Victims of the violence are black and white, rich and poor, young and old, famous and unknown. They are most important of all, human beings whom other human beings loved and needed. No one can be certain who next will suffer from some senseless act of bloodshed, and yet it goes on, and on, and on, in this country of ours. Whenever any American's life is taken by another American unnecessarily, whenever we tear at the fabric of our lives which another man has painfully and clumsily woven for himself and his children, whenever we do this, then the whole nation is degraded. Too often, we honor swagger and bluster and the wielders of force. Too often we excuse those who are willing to build their own lives from the shattered dreams of other human beings. But this much is clear, Violence breeds violence, repression breeds retaliation, and only a cleansing of our whole society can remove this sickness from our souls. For when you teach a man to hate and to fear his brother, when you teach that he is a lesser man because of his color, or his beliefs or the policies that he pursues, when you teach that those who differ from you, threaten your freedom or your job or your home or your family, then you also learn to confront others not as fellow citizens, but as enemies. To be met not with cooperation but with conquest, to be subjugated, and to be mastered. We learn at the last to look at our brothers as aliens. Alien men with whom we share a city, but not a community. Men bound to us in common dwelling, but not in a common effort. We learn to share only a common fear, only a common desire to retreat from each other, only a common impulse to meet disagreement with force. Our lives on this planet are too short, the work to be done is too great. But we can perhaps remember, that those who live with us are our brothers, that they share with us the same short moment of life that they seek as do we, nothing but the chance to live out their lives in purpose and in happiness, surely this bond of common fate, this bond of common roles can begin to teach us something, that we can begin to work a little harder, to become in our hearts brothers and countrymen once again. **Robert F. Kennedy**

The road toward equality of freedom is not easy, and great cost and danger march alongside us. We are committed to peaceful and nonviolent change, and that is important for all to understand — though all change is unsettling. Still, even in the turbulence of protest and struggle is greater hope for the future, as men learn to claim and achieve for themselves the rights formerly petitioned from others. **Robert F. Kennedy**

All do not develop in the same manner, or at the same pace. Nations, like men, often march to the beat of different drummers, and the precise solutions of the United States can neither be dictated nor transplanted to others. What is important is that all nations must march toward increasing freedom; toward justice for all; toward a society strong and flexible enough to meet the demands of all its own people, and a world of immense and dizzying change. **Robert F. Kennedy**

Each nation has different obstacles and different goals, shaped by the vagaries of history and of experience. Yet as I talk to young people around the world I am impressed not by the diversity but by the closeness of their goals, their desires and their concerns and their hope for the future. **Robert F. Kennedy**

I think that we could agree on what kind of a world we would all want to build. it would be a world of independent nations, moving toward international community, each of which protected and respected the basic human freedoms. It would be a world which demanded of each government that it accept its responsibility to insure social justice. It would be a world of constantly accelerating economic progress — not material welfare as an end in itself, but as a means to liberate the capacity of every human being to pursue his talents and to pursue his hopes. It would, in short, be a world that we would be proud to have built. **Robert F. Kennedy**

If we would lead outside our borders, if we would help those who need our assistance, if we would meet our responsibilities to mankind, we must first, all of us, demolish the borders which history has erected between men within our own nations — barriers of race and religion, social class and ignorance. **Robert F. Kennedy**

Our answer is the world's hope; it is to rely on youth. The cruelties and the obstacles of this swiftly changing planet will not yield to obsolete dogmas and outworn slogans. It cannot be moved by those who cling to a present which is already dying, who prefer the illusion of security to the excitement and danger which comes with even the most peaceful progress. This world demands the qualities of youth: not a time of life but a state of mind, a temper of the will, a quality of the imagination, a predominance of courage over timidity, of the appetite for adventure over the love of ease. **Robert F. Kennedy**

First is the danger of futility; the belief there is nothing one man or one woman can do against the enormous array of the world's ills — against misery and ignorance, injustice and violence. Yet many of the world's great movements, of thought and action, have flowed from the work of a single man. A young monk began the Protestant reformation, a young general extended an empire from Macedonia to the borders of the earth, and a young woman reclaimed the territory of France. It was a young Italian explorer who discovered the New World, and 32-year old Thomas Jefferson who proclaimed that all men are created equal. Give me a place to stand, said Archimedes, and I will move the world. These men moved the world, and so can we all. **Robert F. Kennedy**

It is not realistic or hardheaded to solve problems and take action unguided by ultimate moral aims and values, although we all know some who claim that it is so. In my judgment, it is thoughtless folly. For it ignores the realities of human faith and of passion and of belief — forces ultimately more powerful than all of the calculations of our economists or of our generals. Of course to adhere to standards, to idealism, to vision in the face of immediate dangers takes great courage and takes self-confidence. But we also know that only those who dare to fail greatly, can ever achieve greatly. **Robert F. Kennedy**

Like it or not we live in interesting times. They are times of danger and uncertainty; but they are also more open to the creative energy of men than any other time in history. And everyone here will ultimately be judged — will ultimately judge himself — on the effort he has contributed to building a new world society and the extent to which his ideals and goals have shaped that effort. **Robert F. Kennedy**

What it really all adds up to is love -- not love as it is described with such facility in popular magazines, but the kind of love that is affection and respect, order and encouragement, and support. Our awareness of this was an incalculable source of strength, and because real love is something unselfish and involves sacrifice and giving, we could not help but profit from it. Beneath it all, he has tried to engender a social conscience. There were wrongs which needed attention. There were people who were poor and needed help. And we have a responsibility to them and to this country. Through no virtues and accomplishments of our own, we have been fortunate enough to be born in the United States under the most comfortable conditions. We, therefore, have a responsibility to others who are less well off. **Robert F. Kennedy on his father**

What we need in the United States is not division; what we need in the United States is not hatred; what we need in the United States is not violence or lawlessness; but love and wisdom, and compassion toward one another, and a feeling of justice toward those who still suffer within our country, whether they be white or they be black. **Robert F. Kennedy Indianapolis, Indiana, April 4, 1968, announcing to the crowd that Martin Luther King had been assassinated.**

My favorite poet was Aeschylus. He wrote: In our sleep, pain which cannot forget falls drop by drop upon the heart until, in our own despair, against our will, comes wisdom through the awful grace of God. **Robert F. Kennedy, speech on the assassination of Martin Luther King, Jr. April 4, 1968)**

When anyone asks me about the Irish character, I say look at the trees. Maimed, stark and misshapen, but ferociously tenacious. **Edna O'Brien**

There is discrimination in New York, the racial inequality of apartheid in South Africa and serfdom in the mountains of Peru. People starve in the streets of India; a former Prime Minister is summarily executed in the Congo; intellectuals go to jail in Russia; thousands are slaughtered in Indonesia; wealth is lavished on armaments everywhere. These are differing evils; but they are the common works of man. They reflect the imperfection of human justice, the inadequacy of human compassion, the defectiveness of our sensibility toward the sufferings of our fellow human beings at home and around the world. It is these qualities which make of youth today the only true international community. More than this I think that we could agree on what kind of world we want to build. It would be a world of independent nations, moving toward international community, each of which protected and respected basic human freedoms. It would be a world which demanded of each government that it accept its responsibility to insure social justice. It would be a world of constantly accelerating economic progress-not material welfare as an end in itself, but as a means to liberate the capacity of each human being to pursue his talents and his hopes. It would, in short, be a world w would be proud to have built. **Robert F. Kennedy Address, Day of Affirmation, University of Capetown, June 6, 1966.**

Our answer is the world's hope; it is to rely on youth. The cruelties and obstacles of this swiftly changing planet will not yield to obsolete dogmas and outworn slogans. It cannot be moved by those who cling to a present which is already dying, who prefer the illusion of security to the excitement and danger which comes with even the most peaceful progress. This world demands the qualities of youth; not a time of life but a state of mind, a temper of the will, a quality of the imagination, a predominance of courage over timidity, or the appetite for adventure over the love of ease. It is a revolutionary world we live in, and thus, as I have said in Latin America and Asia, in Europe and in the United States, it is young people who must take the lead. Thus you, and your young compatriots everywhere have had thrust upon you a greater burden of responsibility than any generation that has ever lived. **Robert F. Kennedy Address, Day of Affirmation, University of Capetown, June 6, 1966.**

Justice. Justice is land for those who live by farming-and all the world has seen that free farmers on their own land are the surest means to an abundant agriculture. Justice is a decent education for every child-and only with education for all is it possible to create a modern economy...**Statement before Peruvian Students, November, 1965.**

I believe that, as long as there is plenty, poverty is evil. Government belongs wherever evil needs an adversary and there are people in distress who cannot help themselves. **Robert F. Kennedy Speech, Athens, Georgia, May 6, 1961.**

Fear not the path of truth for the lack of people walking on it. **From his last speech, June 5, 1968**

Something about the fact that I made some contribution to either my country, or those who were less well off. I think back to what Camus wrote about the fact that perhaps this world is a world in which children suffer, but we can lessen the number of suffering children, and if you do not do this, then who will do this? I'd like to feel that I'd done something to lessen that suffering. **Interview shortly before he was killed, responding to a question by David Frost about how his obituary should read.**

Being Irish, he had an abiding sense of tragedy, which sustained him through temporary periods of joy. **Brendan Behan**

What's the use of being Irish if the world doesn't break your heart? **John Fitzgerald Kennedy**

Made in the USA
San Bernardino, CA
05 March 2019